MBC

Pot Luck

Cooking and recipes from the past

Jo Lawrie

Illustrations by Peter Bailey

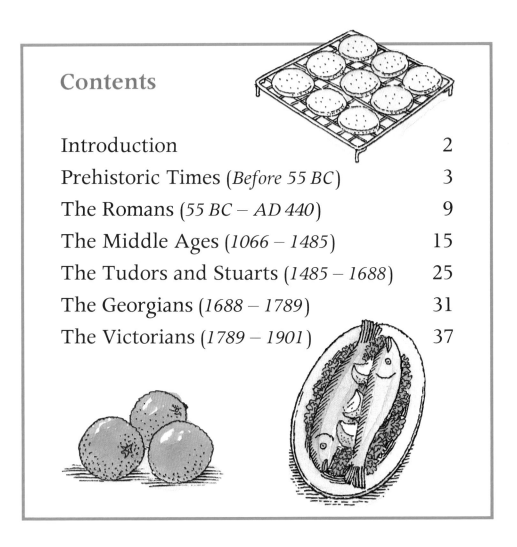

Contents

A & C Black · London

Introduction

When we go shopping in a supermarket we are surrounded by shelves lined with all kinds of food. We can buy canned and 'instant' food in packets, and exotic fresh fruits and vegetables which have been flown in from all over the world. We keep this food fresh in fridges and freezers, then cook it in our microwave ovens or cookers, using water that comes from just turning on the kitchen tap.

Our ancestors did not have such an easy time. They would have been amazed at the choice and plenty in our shops today.

Hundreds of years ago people had to scavenge for food, or try to grow their own crops. Each autumn they had to dry, salt and pickle their food to make it last through the winter. They cooked it over an open fire with water they had probably carried a long way from a well or river.

When did things change and how? This book takes you back to the very earliest times and tells you about food and recipes in Britain from prehistoric times to the Victorian era. Why not go back in time and try some of the recipes for yourself?

Cooking tips

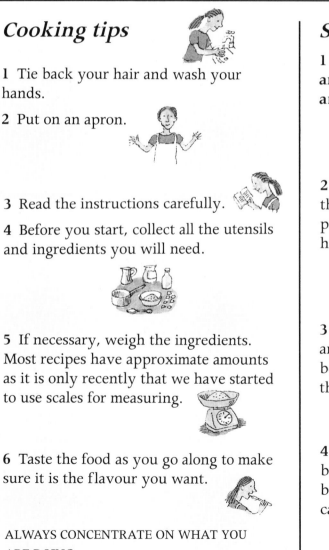

1 Tie back your hair and wash your hands.

2 Put on an apron.

3 Read the instructions carefully.

4 Before you start, collect all the utensils and ingredients you will need.

5 If necessary, weigh the ingredients. Most recipes have approximate amounts as it is only recently that we have started to use scales for measuring.

6 Taste the food as you go along to make sure it is the flavour you want.

ALWAYS CONCENTRATE ON WHAT YOU ARE DOING.

Safety tips

1 **Always make sure an adult is around to watch what you are doing and to help if necessary.**

2 Always use an oven glove to take hot things out of the oven – and make sure pan handles point inwards. Put anything hot on a heat-resistant surface.

3 Some plants are poisonous. If you pick any, check with an adult and a reference book to make sure you have identified them correctly.

4 Never collect fruits or berries from beside a busy road, or where there has been crop-spraying. Always wash food carefully.

Prehistoric Times
(Before 55 BC)

Early in prehistoric times people hunted birds, animals and fish to eat. But they lived mostly on food collected from the local countryside. They were prepared to eat anything – even roots and grubs – in order to stay alive.

Snipe

Thrush

Birds

Some early prehistoric food

Meat

Deer

Fish

Trout

Shellfish

Eggs

Nettles

Plants

Dandelion

Jack by the hedge

Rosehips

Crab apples

Fruit

Raspberries

Berries

Blackberries

Elderberries

The first farmers learned how to clear land and plant crops. They grew wheat, barley, beans and peas, and eventually learned how to grow oats and rye. They made simple oatcakes and used the wheat and rye to make unleavened bread.

Gradually, they learned how to capture wild animals and domesticate them.

They kept cows, sheep and goats in pens to provide them with meat whenever they needed it. When there was milk available they used it to make different kinds of cheese. Sometimes they kept pigs which wandered freely in the forests and hens which were allowed to scratch around and peck in the soil.

3

How did prehistoric people cook?

The people of these times ate their food raw, or cooked over an open fire like this.

They used a sharp stick to hold the food over the flames.

Sometimes larger pieces of meat were cooked in a baking pit.

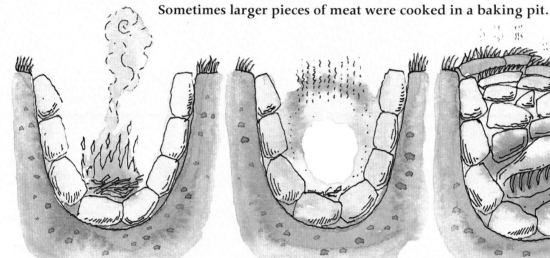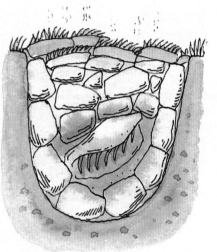

1. A fire was made in a pit lined with stones.

2. When the fire had burned away, the stones were red hot.

3. The food was put on the hot stones and covered by more stones. The pit was sealed with turf to keep in the heat and to bake the food very slowly.

Eventually, people learned to sew animal skins together to make containers. They used these to cook water or broth, bringing the liquid to the boil by adding stones which they had heated in the fire. They also used clay pots for cooking over the fire, or for storing their food.

Utensils

At first people used flint knives and bone or horn spoons to cook with.

Later, when they had discovered how to make bronze and iron, they used these to make sharper knives. They also used metal to make cauldrons, tripods and spits.

How do we know?

'Prehistoric' means 'a time before written history', because there are no written records of what life was like then.

We know about the eating habits of prehistoric times because of the skilful detective work of archaeologists and anthropologists.

There are many ways of finding clues to the past. Archaeologists have discovered charred seeds and impressions on pottery and dug up bones and seashells thrown on to prehistoric rubbish tips. They have also examined the teeth and stomach contents of bodies preserved from that time. Anthropologists have studied primitive communities still in existence to give us more information about how primitive people lived in the past.

▲ A prehistoric cauldron made of metal. It could be balanced on the fire or put on a tripod.

▼ Archaeologists, excavating a Bronze Age skeleton, discovered these stomach contents which include blackberry and rose hip seeds.

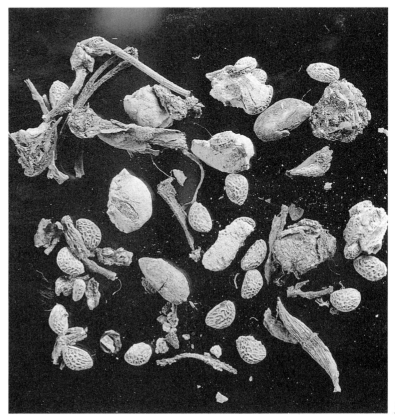

Prehistoric recipes

Cheese

(This needs a few days to complete.)

Ingredients:
1 litre of milk
$\frac{1}{2}$ teaspoon of animal rennet (You can buy this in bottles in most supermarkets)
a pinch of salt
flavourings: pepper, chopped herbs or nettles

What to do:

1 Heat the milk in a pan until tepid (so you can bear to hold your little finger in it quite comfortably).

2 Pour the milk into a wooden or pottery mixing bowl.

3 Stir in the rennet with a wooden spoon.

4 Leave to stand in a warm place until it separates into a white curd in a clear liquid. (This will take about 2 days.)

5 The clear liquid is called whey. Pour this off.

6 Put the curds into a muslin cloth (or fine nylon sieve) to strain. Hang it up to drain (or leave it standing in the sieve).

7 From time to time press the curds to remove as much whey as possible.

8 Mix in the salt, pepper and chopped herbs. You should now have a soft, white cheese which you can serve in a pottery bowl.

If you want to experiment further, you can roll the cheese into a flat cake, wrap it in leaves and bury it in the ground for a couple of weeks to improve the flavour.

Oatcakes

Ingredients:
a lump of animal fat
  (dripping)
4 handfuls of oatmeal
  (plus extra for shaping the oatcakes)
a pinch of salt
a few spoonfuls of water
fat for greasing the baking tray

What to do:

1 Melt the fat in a small saucepan.

2 Mix the oatmeal, salt and melted fat together in a wooden or pottery mixing bowl.

3 Add a little hot water and mix to a fairly soft dough. Work quickly, before the dough gets cold and too stiff to handle.

4 Sprinkle a wooden board with oatmeal to stop the dough from sticking. Take small lumps of dough and quickly flatten each one onto the oatmeal with your hand, until it is about $\frac{1}{4}$ cm thick.

5 Grease a baking tray with some fat and put the oatcakes on it.

6 Bake the oatcakes for 5–10 minutes in a hot oven (about 350°F, 180°C, or Gas Mark 4). While they are cooking look at them from time to time, as they can easily burn.

7 Take them out of the oven and place on a wire tray to cool. Handle them carefully because they are quite fragile.

Nettle soup

(Ask an adult to help you with this.)

Ingredients:
2 marrow bones with lots of meat left on them
enough water to cover these bones in a saucepan
a few pinches of salt
a bundle of nettles
  (cut the young shoots before they start to
  sting and wear rubber gloves when you pick them).
a bunch of 'jack by the hedge' (see page three). If you
  can't find this, use a few chopped herbs eg: parsley,
  thyme or chives

What to do:

1 Put the marrow bones in a saucepan and cover with water. Bring to the boil and leave to simmer (so the water is just bubbling) for several hours.

2 Turn off the heat. When the liquid has cooled to medium heat, strain through a sieve into a large wooden or pottery bowl.

3 Leave it to go cold.

4 Remove the hard layer of fat which has appeared on the top. (Nowadays, many people don't have the time to make stock in this way, so they use a stock cube instead.)

5 Wash the nettles and the 'jack by the hedge' and tear them into small pieces. Throw away any thick pieces of stalk.

6 Pour the cold liquid (this is now called stock as it is full of meaty flavour) into the saucepan and bring to the boil. Put in the nettles and flavouring and leave them to simmer until they are soft and ready to eat.

7 Add a pinch of salt. Taste it to see if it needs more.

8 Serve hot in pottery bowls and eat with bread or the oatcakes from the previous recipe.

Stewed wild fruits

Ingredients:
2 large cooking apples (or 1 cooking apple and a
  handful of crab apples), a handful of blackberries,
  a handful of elderberries
honey
water

What to do:

1 Wash the fruit carefully.

2 Remove stalks and cores.

3 Chop the apples into pieces.

4 Put all the fruit into a saucepan. For each handful of fruit add one dessertspoonful of water. (If you are using crab apples, cook them on their own for about 15 minutes first.)

5 Bring to the boil, and then simmer slowly for about 30 minutes, until the fruit is soft.

6 Add honey to make the fruit as sweet as you like. Eat it hot or cold.

Preserving food

Prehistoric people had to preserve some food to eat in the winter. They did this by salting, smoking or drying the food.

Imagine you have no means of keeping food fresh and try this method of preserving.

Dried apples

Peel and core some apples. Now thread them on a string, either whole or cut into rings. Hang them up to dry in a warm place until you need them. Before using them, soak them in water for 2–3 hours and cook them very slowly in water until soft.

(In prehistoric times the apples were so small they would have been used whole.)

Dried mushrooms

Cut the stalks off some mushrooms. With a darning needle and thread, string the mushroom tops together. Hang them up to dry in a warm place or make a mushroom 'tree' like this one.

Later you can cut the dried mushrooms into strips and add them to soups and stews. They have a good flavour if you simmer them slowly.

Things to do and see

1 Visit Butser Iron Age Farm in Hampshire to learn about the farming and cooking methods of prehistoric people. (Butser Ancient Farm Project, Rookham Lodge, East Meon, Hampshire. Tel: 070 132 386)

2 If you can persuade an adult to help you, why not try preparing and cooking some of the recipes authentically (just as the prehistoric people would have cooked them).

Using a stone quern to grind corn.

The Romans
(55 BC – AD 440)

When the Romans invaded and then ruled over Britain, they introduced many new recipes and methods of cooking. The Roman Empire was very large and covered many lands around the Mediterranean Sea, so the Roman people were often well-travelled and their taste in food was sophisticated. They liked to drink wine, and to eat figs, dates and olives which came by ship from different parts of their Empire. They did not want to eat the coarse bread and drink the ale of the natives of Britain. Wealthy Romans could afford expensive spices which they used to disguise the boring taste of smoked or salted meat and fish.

Unloading a Roman merchant ship at the wharf-side.

Writers of the time described some extraordinary feasts attended by wealthy Romans. One famous Roman, called Trimalchio, held a feast which included wine which was one hundred years old and a wild boar that was stabbed in the belly so that thrushes flew out. During such a feast, guests might eat so much that they had to be sick in a special room, called the 'vomitorium'. Then they would go back into the dining room and continue eating.

A Roman kitchen

This type of kitchen would have been in use in Britain soon after the Roman conquest (certainly by about AD 100). It was a great improvement on cooking around an open fire.

Cooking utensils are made of wood, bone, iron or bronze.

The gridiron supports the cooking pot and frying pan.

Storage jars.

Special container, with holes and ridges, used for fattening edible dormice. The dormice were fed on walnuts, acorns and chestnuts. They were considered a great delicacy.

A Roman dining room (AD 200)

The Roman dining room was called a triclinium. The Romans who ate in this kind of room were the civilians sent from Rome to rule over the British towns, and the wealthy people who had settled in villas and were farming the surrounding land. Guests may have included a few Britains, who would have been of a high social class.

The main meals of the day were:
1 A light breakfast of bread and fruit.
2 Prandium (lunch) – a cold meal of eggs, fish or vegetables
3 Cena – the evening dinner and main meal of the day.

The three courses at dinner were:
Gustatio – tasty things like radishes or asparagus to tempt the appetite.
Primae mensae – the meat course, which might include chicken or hare and would also have fish and vegetable dishes.
Secundae mensae – the sweet course, which included fruit.

The Romans ate mainly with their fingers, using napkins to wipe them clean.

They used spoons for eating soft foods and sauces, and knives for cutting and spearing meat.

Roman food and recipes

A famous Roman, called Apicius, wrote a cookery book called 'De Re Quoquinaria' ('The Art of Cooking'). Many of his recipes are very exotic, such as stuffed dormice and snails fattened in milk. He does not give accurate measurements but instructions like 'as much as you can hold between finger and thumb'.

You can start your Roman cookery with a more everyday dish.

Cooked peas
(These can be eaten hot or cold.)

Ingredients:
3 handfuls of dried peas
small onion, chopped
one dessertspoon wine vinegar
one dessertspoon olive oil
2 hardboiled eggs
salt and pepper

What to do:

Soak the dried peas overnight in a bowl of water. Simmer them (cook slowly) in a pan until soft and stir in some finely chopped onion. Season to taste with salt and pepper. Make a dressing of wine vinegar and oil. Pour it over the peas. Decorate with hardboiled eggs.

Roman bread was often unleavened (contained no yeast and therefore did not rise), so if you eat your peas with pitta bread, you will be eating in true Roman style!

This photograph shows bread which was left ▶ behind at Pompeii (a Roman town near Naples, which was destroyed by a volcano in AD 79). Nowadays, in Pompeii museum you can see eggs, hazelnuts, almonds, dates and a loaf of bread. They were all preserved by the molten lava which engulfed the town.

▼ The main foods for ordinary Roman citizens were bread and porridge. They also liked vegetables and fruit, eggs and cheese. The Romans always used honey for sweetening and herbs for flavouring.

Here are some more Roman recipes you may like to try.

Dates cooked in honey

(You should have an adult around to supervise the use of
a sharp knife.)

Ingredients:
12 fresh dates
12 walnut halves
enough honey to fry the dates
salt
ground black pepper

What to do:

1 Peel the skins from the dates with a sharp knife. On a chopping
board, cut along one side of each date, and take out the stone.

2 Put a walnut half into each date.

3 Sprinkle the dates lightly with salt.

4 Put them into a pan and fry gently in honey for about 5 minutes.

5 Lift the dates out with a spoon, and arrange on a serving dish.

6 Spoon some more honey on top and sprinkle lightly with the
ground black pepper.

The Romans particularly liked to drink wine. Try this recipe
for spiced wine (using grape juice instead of wine).

Spiced wine

Ingredients:
1 litre grape juice
2 dessertspoons honey
a large pinch of each of these
spices: mixed spice, nutmeg,
cinnamon, ground black pepper
(you could grind the pepper
yourself with a pestle and mortar,
to find out how long it takes)
water

What to do:

1 Pour the grape juice into a 'Roman-looking' jug
and dilute with water until it is the right strength for
your taste (half and half might be about right).

2 Stir in the honey with a wooden spoon, until it is
sweet enough.

3 Sprinkle the spices and pepper into the jug and
stir. Taste it and add more if necessary.

Numidian chicken

(You should have an adult around to help you with this recipe and to supervise the use of the oven.)

Ingredients:
1 prepared chicken with guts removed
a few pinches of ground black pepper
olive oil for cooking

For the sauce:
a pinch of ground pepper
a pinch of ground cumin
a pinch of coriander seeds
a handful of chopped nuts and chopped dates
1 dessertspoon olive oil
2 dessertspoons grape juice
1 teaspoon wine vinegar
broth (you could use a chicken stock cube)
honey to taste
a handful of breadcrumbs

What to do:

1 Put the chicken in a roasting tin and sprinkle it with ground black pepper and olive oil.

2 Roast the chicken in a fairly hot oven (350°F, 180°C, Gas Mark 4) for 1–1½ hours, basting occasionally (spooning the hot oil over the top of the chicken to stop it from drying out). Ask an adult to do this for you.

Roast the chicken until it is golden brown and until the juices are colourless rather than pink. (You can test this by pricking the chicken with a fork.)

3 Put all the sauce ingredients into a saucepan and simmer over a low heat, stirring occasionally, for about 20 minutes.

4 Put the cooked chicken onto a serving dish, pour the hot sauce over it, and sprinkle it with ground black pepper.

Things to do and see

1 Visit the Corinium Museum at Cirencester in Gloucester, or the Museum of London. In both museums you can see a life-size reconstruction of a Roman kitchen and a Roman dining room.

2 Hold your own Roman feast. Dress up like Roman men and women, wearing togas and Roman hairstyles and head-dresses.

You can find lots more Roman recipes in the books listed below:

Food and Cooking in Roman Britain by Marion Woodman (obtainable from Corinium Museum, Cirencester, Gloucestershire)

Food and Cooking in Roman Britain by Jane Renfrew (published by English Heritage)

The Middle Ages
(1066 – 1485)

The Romans had left Britain by the 5th Century AD and, for several centuries afterwards, the ordinary British people existed much as they had done before the Roman invasion, and once again became self-sufficient. They kept cows, pigs and hens and grew a few vegetables; sometimes they went out hunting for birds or rabbits, or fished in the rivers and streams.

▲ Medieval bakers at work.

▲ Milking a cow by hand (taken from a medieval manuscript).

Most people went to the local mill to grind their flour, and baked loaves of coarse bread. Everybody, including the children, drank home-brewed ale.

If the weather was bad and the crops failed, everyone suffered. Some people starved or were forced to grind up acorns to make flour, boil grass and roots to make pottage (a kind of thick soup) and sometimes even to eat rats!

Only the rich could afford to drink wine and eat fine white bread. A few, very wealthy people could afford to hold great feasts.

In 1467 great celebrations were held in honour of Archbishop Neville of York. The feast included 104 oxen, 400 swans, 2,000 geese, 1,500 hot pasties of venison, 12 porpoises, 300 quarters of wheat and 13,000 dishes of jellies, cold tarts and custards. This was washed down with 100 tunnes of wine!

A medieval banquet

At a feast table manners were very important. Most people, even kings and queens, ate with their fingers, so there were certain rules to be obeyed . . .

'He who . . . pokes about on the platter (searching presumably for the best bits of food) is unpleasant and annoys his neighbour at dinner.'

The marshal organised the seating with the most important guests at the top table, 'above the salt'. Everyone washed their hands in scented water and the bread and salt was tasted to check it was not poisoned. Every guest had a 'trencher' or slice of bread in their place.

A trumpeter sounded the fanfare and the steward led in a procession of servants carrying the first course. Between the different courses a servant carried round an alms bowl to collect food for the poor.

Whenever a guest had finished gnawing on a bone, they were supposed to throw it on the floor rather than put it back in the dish from which it was served.

'If it happen that you cannot help scratching (perhaps at a louse) then courteously take a portion of your dress, and scratch with that. It is more befitting than that your skin should become soiled.'

'Do not touch the salt in the salter cellar with any meat; but lay salt honestly on your trencher for that is courtesy.'

'Before meals it is right to wash your hands openly, even though you have no need to do so, in order that those who dip their fingers in the same dish as yourself may know for certain that you have cleaned them.'

Subtleties

These were magnificent creations made of marzipan, pastry, fondant or jelly. They were carried into a banquet between courses, to be either admired or eaten. They helped to fill the time whilst servants brought the next course from the kitchen.

Cooking improvements

For centuries people had cooked their food over an open fire, which was in the middle of the floor. There was a hole in the roof for the smoke and fumes to go out, but the homes of ordinary people were very stuffy and smoky.

Those who could afford to live in castles and large houses changed the position of the fire to the side wall, and built chimneys above for the smoke to get out.

There was no electricity, and no tinned or packet foods, so every single ingredient had to be prepared by hand. Cooking large, tasty meals was very time-consuming, so rich people had many servants to work in the kitchens.

A castle kitchen in medieval times

Hanging on the wall were pans, scoops, ladles and gridirons which were used for cooking.

A rough wooden table and a chopping block – used for cutting up vegetables, meat and bones. Many recipes of the time instructed the cook to 'smite hem to gobbets'.

Near the fire they kept pokers, tongs and bellows to control the flames.

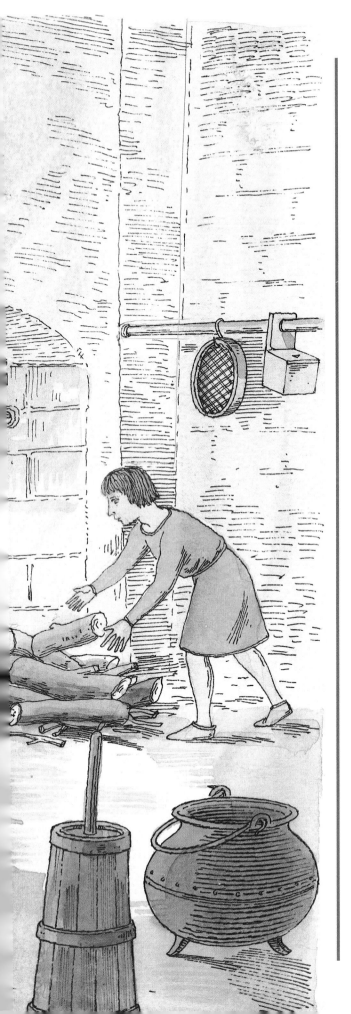

'Pot luck'

There are some interesting phrases that we still use nowadays, which originated in the Middle Ages.

When a cauldron or pot of soup was cooking over the fire, a guest might be offered a ladleful. If they were lucky the offering might include some bits of meat – if not, they might have had to be satisfied with a taste of barley or a turnip. The guest had to take 'pot luck' and accept whatever came out of the pot.

The expressions 'above' and 'below the salt' referred to the position of a guest at table. Salt was very expensive and was served in a decorative container, placed in front of the chief guest. Therefore, important people sat 'above' the salt, and the less important sat 'below' it.

At a medieval feast, the pantler (whose job it was to serve the bread) would cut off the upper crust and offer it to the chief guest. We still use the phrase 'upper crust' to refer to important people in society.

19

Spicing and preserving food for the winter

Medieval cooks kept salt handy in a saltbox on the wall, and locked away expensive items such as spices, almonds, dried fruits and sugar. The main spices at that time were ginger, pepper, cloves, cinnamon, mace and galingale. These spices came to Europe in ships from the East and were used a great deal in the winter to vary the flavour of preserved meat.

In the winter months there was virtually no fresh food to feed animals, so only a few were kept alive for breeding. The others were killed for meat. As there were no fridges or freezers, the people preserved food by salting, smoking or drying it.

A wooden salt box.

▲ A man warms himself as a cooking pot simmers on the fire. Notice the pig and the sausages which are being smoked to preserve them.

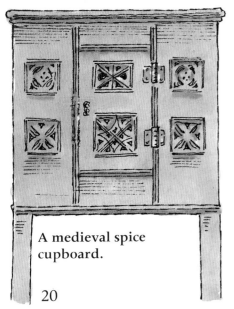

A medieval spice cupboard.

When the time came to eat the salted food, the cook had to soak it several times in fresh water to remove the salt. Even so, the food often still had a very salty flavour.

The medieval church forbade people to eat meat on Fridays and saints' days, so they ate fish regularly. Sometimes they ate dried stockfish which came from Norway, although they had to beat this to a paste with a sledge hammer before it was fit to cook!

20

Medieval food and recipes

There are some famous medieval cookery books which still exist today such as '*The Forme of Cury*', first printed in 1390. Like the Roman recipes, they do not give accurate amounts of ingredients, but phrases such as 'cast thereto wine enough'. Often we have to make a guess at how much of something to put in, and whether or not the taste we have produced is authentic.

In the Middle Ages the spices would have lost some of their flavour after a long journey from the East. Also, the fruit and vegetables of those times were small and wizened, very unlike the huge shiny items on display in our supermarkets nowadays. Eggs were much smaller, and animals were more scraggy and tough than those of today.

Shopkeepers weren't as careful about the way they kept and prepared food as they are now. In 1316, two London bakers were charged with making bread of 'false, putrid and rotten materials' and others sold loaves which were underweight. Sellers of ale often watered it down and fishmongers often tried to sell stale fish.

Important ingredients for medieval recipes

Before starting to cook medieval food it is useful to learn how to make four basic ingredients, which appear in many recipes. They are: verjuice, poudre fort, poudre douce and almond milk.

Verjuice – juice of crab apples or green grapes, sometimes mixed with honey and spices (lemon juice will do instead).

Poudre fort (strong powder) – this was 'hot', probably made of ginger, pepper, cinnamon, mace, allspice, cloves and dried chives.

Poudre douce (sweet powder) – was milder and no doubt included spices such as ground aniseed, fennel seed, cinnamon and nutmeg.

Almond milk – to make this, pour hot water over some ground almonds and stir in a pinch of salt and honey until it is sweet as you like it. Leave to stand for 30 minutes, stirring occasionally. Add some white grape juice according to your taste.

Pottage

This is what the poorer people lived on most of the time, adding whatever flavourings and scraps of food were available, including chopped herbs which everyone grew on their plot of land.

Ingredients:
2 handfuls whole wheat or barley grains

What to do:

Soak the wheat or barley overnight in water. The next day simmer gently in a saucepan until soft. Add flavourings.

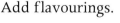

Rastons

(This is a surprise dish. The loaf is meant to look untouched so that the filling is unexpected. Ask an adult to help you with this recipe.)

Ingredients:
1 white, round loaf
a large knob of butter
1 tablespoon of crushed fennel or poppy seeds
1 tablespoon poudre douce
raisins (optional)

What to do:

1 With a breadknife, cut the top of the loaf off with a zigzag cut, in the way you cut a pumpkin for Halloween.

2 Put the top crust to one side.

3 Scoop out the bread from the bottom half of the loaf and crumble it.

4 Melt the butter over a low heat in a large pan. Toss the breadcrumbs in the butter.

5 Add all the spices, flavourings and the raisins.

6 Put the spiced crumbs in the loaf and replace the top crust.

7 Re-heat in a moderate oven for a few minutes before serving. (350°F, 180°C, Gas Mark 4)

Blank-mang

This is very different from the blancmange we know nowadays.
It was very popular in the Middle Ages.

Ingredients:

2 chicken breasts with no fat attached
$\frac{1}{4}$ litre of almond milk (see page 21)
a knob of butter
1 dessertspoon of honey

1 cupful of rice
whole almonds
parsley sprigs
salt to taste

What to do:

1 Simmer the chicken breasts in the almond milk in a covered pan for 15 minutes.

2 Using a sieve, strain the broth from the chicken pieces into a bowl. Put the chicken pieces on one side to cool slightly.

3 Return the broth to the saucepan and put in the rice, knob of butter and honey. Now cook the rice until it is done.

4 While the rice is cooking, shred the chicken into small pieces, removing any skin or bone.

5 Mix the chicken and the cooked rice together and return to the stove to re-heat the chicken thoroughly. Stir well so that it does not burn.

6 Lay on a dish and garnish with the whole almonds and parsley to serve.

Urchins

Ingredients:

500 gms minced pork
2 tablespoons breadcrumbs
1 tablespoon poudre fort

1 beaten egg
sliced almonds (if possible dyed either green,
   yellow, or red with food colouring)
fat to grease the frying pan and the baking tin

What to do:

1 Mix the pork, breadcrumbs, seasonings and egg in a bowl.

2 Flour your hands and roll small lumps of the mixture into balls.

3 Cover each ball in flour and brown the outside in a well-greased frying pan.

4 Transfer the meat balls into a well-greased baking tin and put into a medium-heat oven (about 375°F, 190°C, Gas Mark 5). Cook for 30 minutes.

5 Remove from the oven and quickly stick the slivered almonds into each ball so it looks like a hedgehog. Serve hot.

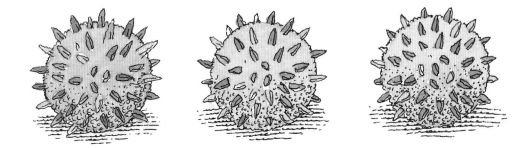

Pokerounce

Ingredients:
10 fingers of toast
2 tbsps of clear honey
a small pinch of ground black pepper
a large pinch of ground ginger
a large pinch of cinnamon
pine nuts for garnish

What to to:

1 Put the honey and spices in a small pan and heat gently for 3 or 4 minutes.

2 Pour the honey mixture on to the toast fingers and spread it.

3 Decorate each toast finger with a few pine nuts.

Hippocras

This was a spiced wine drunk after the meal by people of high station when they retired to the chamber.

Ingredients:
1 litre red grape juice (instead of wine)
a pinch of ginger
a pinch of cinnamon
a pinch of grains of paradise (not available now,
   so use crushed cardamon pods instead)
a dessertspoonful of sunflower seeds
a dessertspoonful of orange peel
sugar or honey to taste

What to do:

1 Put all the ingredients into a saucepan.

2 Heat and strain before serving.

3 Adjust the sweetness to your own taste, but do not make it too sweet or you will not notice the other flavours.

Retiring with a goblet of spiced wine.

24

Things to do

Create your own medieval feast!

Use the recipes and ideas in this section of the book to help you – and here are some books that you may find useful:

A Medieval Feast by Aliki (The Bodley Head)

The Merry Company Books 1 & 2 by A & M Bagenal (O.U.P.)

Food and Cooking In Medieval Britain by M Black (English Heritage)

Medieval Holidays and Festivals by M Penlar Cosman (Piatkus)

The Tudors and the Stuarts
(1485 – 1688)

During the 16th and 17th centuries there were many improvements in cooking methods and new ingredients, such as potatoes, were used.

Cooks of this time still used cauldrons hanging over an open fire, but they were able to adjust the heat from the fire by two new ideas: the pot crane and the ratchet. The ratchet meant that the pot could be raised or lowered. The pot crane could swing above the hottest part of the fire or be moved away in order to simmer the contents of the pot.

A brushwood fire was lit inside the bake oven to heat it. Then the ashes were raked out. The food was sealed inside the oven and baked slowly in the heat given out from the stones.

A Tudor kitchen

Pot crane

Ratchet

The meat was fitted onto spikes or placed in a metal basket in front of the fire.

Spit for roasting resting on fire dogs.

Skillet

A young boy, called a turnspit, often had the job of turning the spit so that the meat cooked evenly.

Eating habits

During this time eating habits changed. Wealthy families often dined in a small chamber rather than in the main hall.

Tableware was more hygenic, and instead of wooden trenchers, people began to use plates of glazed earthenware pottery, or pewter.

The poorer people used horn beakers and leatherjacks, and the rich had utensils made of silver, gold and Venetian glass. The pewter spoons used were pear-shaped, and knives were rounded at the ends as they no longer had to be pointed to spear meat. Forks were still not very common, although they were used in other parts of Europe.

▲ A Stuart dining room in the Castle Museum, York.

Leather jack

Pewter plate and spoon

Glass goblet

Water carrier

Drinks

Beer became as popular as ale as an everyday drink. Fresh water was a luxury and had to be brought from the water seller who carried barrels around the street.

Ice house

This was another new idea which reached Britain in the 17th century. In the winter a deep pit was dug and packed with blocks of ice and layers of straw. The pit was covered in a stone roof which insulated it, and so it kept cool during the summer months (as long as the weather was not too hot).

Ice house

26

Voyages of exploration

From Tudor times, European sailors began to go on longer voyages of exploration around the world. They discovered many new things which changed people's eating habits, such as potatoes and tomatoes, and more readily available sugar.

The explorers brought back new drinks too. Amongst these were coffee, tea and chocolate.

There was always a shortage of fresh water on board ship, and the lack of fresh fruit and vegetables caused many sailors to die of a disease called scurvy. The main food was salted meat and fish, and a special ship's biscuit which remained edible for fifty years. One of the sailors describes how 'the biscuit was so full of worms that, God help me, I saw many wait until nightfall to eat the porridge made of it so as not to see the worms.'

Over the years sailors discovered how to preserve food in other ways. They learned how to make stock cubes which would keep for years and dissolve in hot water to make soup. They potted meat and sealed the top with suet, and they grew watercress in jars.

Gardening

During the sixteenth and seventeenth centuries there was a great interest in gardening, and many fruits were cultivated. These included quinces, apricots, peaches, nectarines, figs, cherries, raspberries and blackcurrants. In 1665, Charles II was presented with the first pineapple ever to be grown in Britain!

A formal garden dating from this time.

Gardens were laid out in very formal designs with the beds arranged symmetrically. They included lots of herbs and flowers, such as marigolds, which were often included in salads. As well as supervising the cooking, the mistress of a large house would be expected to know about herbal remedies and the cure of the sick.

Sixteenth and seventeenth century recipes

▼ A cookery book from 1677

Recipe books of the time, such as 'The Good huswife's Jewell' and 'The Closet of Sir Kenelm Digby Opened' inform us that pies were very popular. Mince pie was a favourite, containing meat as well as dried fruits and spices.

Mince pie

(This recipe assumes the cook knows how to make pastry. You could use frozen pastry if you like.)

Ingredients:
350 gms of shortcrust
200 gms of raisins
a teaspoon of mixed spice
250 gms of minced beef
egg yolk
fat to grease the baking tin

What to do:

1 Make a 'coffin' of pastry (line a greased baking tin with pastry and bake it 'blind' by pricking it with a fork and then part-baking it.) The 'coffin' can be any shape. Bake 'blind' at Gas Mark 7, 425°F, 220°C for 15 minutes.

2 Put the mixed spice, raisins and minced meat into a mixing bowl and stir. Put the mixture into the 'coffin'.

3 Roll out a pastry lid and place it on top of the pie.

4 Make a design for the lid with the remaining bits of pastry.

5 Brush the top with egg yolk so that it is golden and shiny when cooked.

6 Bake for 45 minutes in a moderate oven (350°F, 180°C, Gas Mark 4).

'A tarte with hid jewels'
(An egg custard, with fruit, in 'a coffin')

Ingredients:
250 gms of shortcrust pastry
200 gms of red fruit eg. raspberries or strawberries (these are the jewels)
3 eggs
140 mls of cream
430 mls of milk

What to do:

1 Make a 'coffin' as above and bake it 'blind' at 425°F, 220°C, Gas Mark 7 for about 15 minutes.

2 Half-fill the tart with the red fruit.

3 Beat the eggs with the milk and cream in a mixing bowl.

4 Pour this over the fruit and bake in a moderate oven (350°F, 180°C, Gas Mark 4) for about 40 minutes until it is set.

28

Crystallised rose petals

(These were a delicacy to eat or just used as decoration.)

Ingredients:
rose petals
1 egg white
3–4 tablespoons of caster sugar

What to do:

1 Pick some rose petals and check that they are clean and dry.

2 Brush each petal with a thin coating of beaten egg white and sprinkle with caster sugar, making sure that it is well covered.

3 Leave to dry on a sheet of greaseproof paper on a wire baking tray, then store in an airtight container.

Marchpane (marzipan)

Ingredients:
6 cupfuls of ground almonds
3 cupfuls of icing sugar
  (and some extra in case the
  mixture turns out too sticky)
white of an egg
food colouring

What to do:

1 Put the ground almonds, icing sugar and beaten egg into a bowl. Mix to a firm paste.

2 Divide into three portions, leaving one as it is and using food colouring to make one portion pink, and the other green.

3 Using more icing sugar to stop the marzipan from sticking, make the shape of a Tudor Rose on a wooden board. (You could also make some marzipan fruits and arrange them in a small basket.)

Stuffed apricots

(You can buy semi-hydrated apricots which are best for this; dried apricots are not as easy to use.)

Ingredients:
semi-hydrated apricots
cream cheese
walnuts

What to do:

1 Slit open the apricots with a knife.

2 Stuff them with cream cheese.

3 Decorate each with half a walnut, and serve.

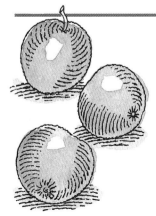

Pippin water

1 Chop some windfall apples into chunks, including the cores and the skin.

2 Cover with water and simmer them for about half an hour.

3 Strain everything through a sieve and add honey, lemon juice and more water to taste.

A Fysshe with a pudding in its belly

Ingredients:

a fish (eg. trout)
a handful of breadcrumbs
a handful of chopped bacon
a handful of chopped parsley

$\frac{1}{4}$ teaspoon of salt
a large pinch of ground black pepper
parsley and lemon for decoration
oil

What to do:

1 Ask a grown-up to help you slit the fish along the belly and remove the guts. Rinse clean.

2 Stuff the belly with a mixture of breadcrumbs, bacon, parsley and seasoning.

3 Brush a baking tray with the oil and place the fish on it. Sprinkle oil on the fish and bake for about 20 minutes in a medium oven (350°F, 180°C, Gas Mark 4).

4 Arrange the fish on a serving dish and decorate with parsley and slices of lemon.

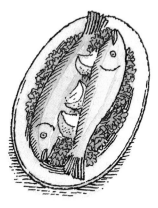

Things to do

Posy mats

These were used as plates for sticky puddings. When the guest had finished eating, he turned his posy mat over to find something amusing written on the other side. The posy mats above were made of earthenware pottery with a tin glaze. After a meal each mat was turned over and the rhyme was read out. One of these says 'THE ROSE IS RED. THE LEAVES ARE GREEN. GOD SAVE ELIZABETH, OUR QUEENE'.

Try making your own posy mats out of cardboard. Think of some other rhymes to put on them.

Make a herb garden

Try planting your own herb garden. Start with the more well-known herbs such as sage, parsley, rosemary and thyme. Then find out about more unusual ones such as comfrey and borage.

A useful book is: ***Herbs in Pots***, by Polly Pinder, published by Search Press, Wellwood, North Farm Road, Tunbridge Wells, Kent TN2 3DR.
(This tells you how to grow herbs and how to use them in cooking and medicine.)

The Georgians
(1688 – 1789)

Agricultural improvements and inventions

During this time, there were many new ideas for improving crop growing and the rearing of animals. A man called Jethro Tull invented a seed drill which sowed the seeds in a more efficient way than the old method of scattering seeds by hand.

The idea of growing clover and turnips to provide winter fodder for the animals meant that they did not have to be killed in the autumn. This made fresh meat more available.

▼ Jethro Tull's seed drill. Seed was put into the wooden hoppers and dribbled out in two rows. This made it much easier to weed the fields later in the season.

▲ Thomas Coke held an annual sheep-shearing festival at Holkham in Norfolk. Many new breeds of animal were developed, and amongst these were sheep which Coke sold to farmers all over Europe.

A new law had been passed to make farming more efficient in order to meet the needs of a growing population. All the agricultural land was 'enclosed' into big fields owned by wealthy farmers. This meant that the poor countryfolk could no longer grow their crops on strips of land or keep their cows on the 'common' land, as this had now disappeared.

It became more and more difficult for the peasant farmers to live, and many moved to the towns and cities to look for a different sort of work.

Food markets

The biggest food markets were in London. Animals from all over the country were driven there 'on the hoof'. Cattle driven from Anglesey, in Wales, even had to swim across the Menai Straits.

Many of the roads were improved at this time which meant it was easier to bring fresh fruit and vegetables to Covent Garden market each day, as well as fresh fish to Billingsgate market

Street traders

All sorts of street traders were a common sight in the eighteenth century. They each called out in a special way to attract custom.

The vinegar boy had two barrels of vinegar slung across his donkey's back.

The potato seller was often accompanied by a child who helped fill the housewives' baskets.

The herb wife – people of that time used herbs for a variety of things.

Milkmaids went round the streets with churns and ladled the mik into the customer's own container. Milk bought in this way could be a health hazard. A writer of the time tells us . . .

'The milk . . . (was) carried through the streets in open pails, exposed to foul rinsings discharged from doors and windows, spittle . . . from foot passengers; overflowings from mudcarts, spatterings from coach wheels, dirt and trash chucked into it by rogueish boys for the joke's sake . . .'

Milkmaids carried milk churns slung by leather straps ▶
from a wooden yoke.

Sally Lunn

Sally Lunn was supposed to have been a well-known street seller in Bath. She sold a type of tea-cake, which you can still buy there nowadays. If you would like to try one, why not make your own?

Recipe for Sally Lunns

Ingredients:
190 mls of milk
a knob of butter
12 heaped tablespoons of plain flour (warmed)
$\frac{1}{2}$ teaspoon of salt
1 egg
25 gms of fresh yeast
1 tablespoon of sugar dissolved
  in a tablespoon of milk (this is for glazing the teacakes)
lard for greasing the cake tins

What to do:

1 Heat the milk in a pan and dissolve the butter in it. Let it cool until you can hold your little finger in it comfortably.

2 Put the egg into a small bowl and beat it. Mix it with some of the lukewarm milk.

3 Cream the fresh yeast and sugar together in another bowl, and add to the egg and milk.

4 Sift the warmed flour and the salt through the sieve into a large mixing bowl. Make a well (hollow) in the middle of the flour and pour in the liquid. Mix the flour to a soft

dough. Turn it on to a floured board and knead it (keep bringing the sides to the middle) for a few minutes.

5 Put half the dough in one warmed, greased tin and half in another. Cover with a cloth. Leave in a warm place for about 30 minutes until the dough has doubled in size.

6 Bake in a ready-warmed oven (at about 425°F, 218°C, Gas Mark 7) for about 25 minutes. Brush with the glaze and return to the oven for a few minutes to dry.

7 Serve sliced and toasted, and spread with butter.

33

Eating habits

During the eighteenth century there was still a great difference between the food eaten by the rich and the poor.

There were many poor people in the towns, and they lived in cold, miserable homes, which were often very crowded. Their diet was mainly bread, potatoes and beer, with perhaps an egg, some cheese, fish or meat as a treat.

▲ The poor begged for scraps from servants of wealthy households.

▼ An eighteenth-century glutton tucks into a hearty meal.

The rich ate meals of several courses with a great many dishes for each course. Cooks used more sugar and spices were used less.

A Norfolk parson of the time, the Reverend James Woodforde wrote in his diary about a sumptuous dinner which took place when he was appointed pro-proctor at Oxford.

'The first course was, part of a large Cod, a chine of Mutton, some Soup, a Chicken Pye, Pudding and Roots etc. Second course, Pidgeons and Asparagus, a Fillet of Veal with Mushrooms and high Sauce with it, rosted Sweetbreads, hot Lobster, Apricot Tart and in the middle a Pyramid of Syllabub and Jellies. We had a Dessert of Fruit after Dinner, and Madeira, White Port and red to drink as Wine. We were all very merry and cheerful.'

Meals were also laid out in a more elegant way, with silver and china plates. Men and women no longer sat grouped at opposite ends of the table, but sat alternately, so that the men could attend to the women's needs.

Drinks

In the early part of the century the wealthy drank coffee and chocolate, and coffee houses were fashionable. However, these drinks were expensive and were drunk less as tea gradually became more popular.

At first tea was very expensive and only the rich could afford to drink it, but by the end of the century even the poor people drank tea. A working man's family was prepared to spend £2 of its £40 a year income on cheap tea and sugar.

▲ A wealthy family takes tea.

▲ A woman cooking on a hob grate.

Cooking improvements

A new kind of small grate called the 'hob' grate was invented at this time. Coal was now quite a common fuel and as it had a much hotter flame than other fuel, a smaller fire was adequate. The grate was made of cast iron and had a fire box raised from the ground. There were two iron surfaces on which pans or kettles could stand and extra 'trivets' swung out from the fire, which were used to keep things simmering.

The hob grate was an important invention because cooking was no longer quite such heavy work, and so more women were able to take charge of the kitchens.

Drinks recipes from the Georgian era

Other drinks at this time were hot punch in the winter, and fruit cordials and sherbets in the summer.
Here are some recipes for drinks you might like to try.

A non-alcoholic punch

Ingredients:
2 litres of apple juice
6 large oranges
sugar to taste (about 2 tablespoons)
a teaspoon of ground cinnamon
ground nutmeg
whole cloves
$1\frac{3}{4}$ litres of water

What to do:

Chop up the oranges into rough hunks and simmer in $1\frac{3}{4}$ litres of water with the sugar and the spices. After about thirty minutes, strain everything through a sieve and heat up in a large pan with the apple juice.

Elderflower cordial

Ingredients:
20 elderflower heads
  (or you could use dried elderflowers, which can be bought in health shops)
8 tablespoons of sugar
2 lemons

What to do:

Shake the elderflower heads free of any insects. Put the flower heads in a large pan of boiled, cooled water. Dissolve eight tablespoons of sugar in the water and slice in two lemons. Leave to stand for 24 hours stirring occasionally. Strain and serve diluted, according to taste.

Strawberry sherbet

Ingredients:
2 punnets of washed strawberries
juice of one lemon
juice of one orange
4 tablespoons of caster sugar

What to do:

Crush the strawberries to a smooth mash and add the lemon and orange juice. Leave to stand for about 3 hours. Put the caster sugar into a bowl and strain the fruit on to it, through a sieve. This will make sherbet, which you should serve chilled, in a small glass with a lump of ice.

Things to do and see

1 Many stately homes date from this period and often the most interesting room is the kitchen. See if there is one you can visit near to where you live.

2 A local rural life museum will probably include a display about dairying. If you are lucky, there might be a demonstration of butter churning or cheese making.

3 Write and illustrate your own eighteenth-century recipe book.
(Use the books recommended on page 48 to help you.)

The Victorians
(1789 – 1901)

During the nineteenth century, many new developments improved the quality of cooking – especially in wealthier homes.

By 1900 most towns were linked by a railway network. This meant that goods could be distributed much more quickly and cheaply, so a wider choice of food became available at lower prices. Milk, eggs and cheese were much fresher when brought from the country by rail, and meat sent by rail was better quality than meat from animals that had previously been driven along the roads.

▲ After 1880, cheap frozen meat and fish could be transported from abroad in the newly developed refrigerated steamships.

▼ Packaged food at the turn of the century.

▲ An early advertisement for Heinz baked beans.

Food was more closely checked for standards of safety. This was because there had been many cases of 'adulteration' of food, when shopkeepers cheated the customers by watering down their milk, putting sand in the sugar or selling used tea leaves over again.

More and more tinned goods became available. To begin with, only meat and fish were sold in tins, but by 1890 people could buy tinned vegetables and fruit. In 1895, Heinz baked beans were invented.

37

Markets and street sellers were partly replaced by better quality food stores, such as J Sainsbury. These shops advertised their produce and sold food in a cleaner, more hygenic way.

Factories mass produced cooking stoves, crockery, cutlery and kitchen equipment which made life easier for a cook. The new stoves burned coal in a smaller grate and although these could sometimes be tricky to use, people were able to control the heat and use it more effectively. Families who had no stoves could send their dinners and pies to the 'bakehouse' to be cooked.

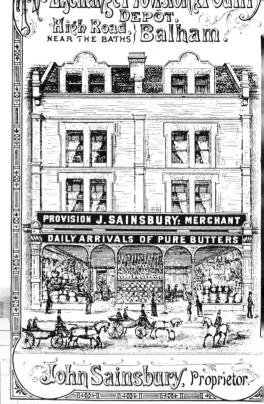

▲ The stores stressed the cleanliness and safety of their products and their staff wore crisp, white overalls.

▲ A Victorian kitchen range.

One of Mrs Beeton's ▶ popular cookery books.

Also, there were many cookery books written and published at this time. Mrs Beeton's 'Book of Household Management' was a bestseller and, along with Eliza Acton's 'Modern Cookery for Private Families', is still used today.

Rich and poor

By the end of the nineteenth century, many of the peasant farmers and farm labourers had moved to the towns to find work. Living conditions for the poor in towns were very low indeed. Factory workers laboured for long hours for little pay, and lived mainly on cheap white bread, porridge and tea, with bacon at the weekend. A vegetable broth was thought to be a filling meal.

Conditions were not much better for those who had stayed in the country, although some families could grow a few vegetables or keep a pig. An old man recalls, 'Many a time I hunted and foraged about for snails in the hedges and roasted them for my lunch or tea.'

A railwayman's wife at work in her kitchen. Not everyone could afford the new cast iron grate and many people still cooked over an open fire.

The poverty and hunger among factory workers was so appalling that charitable organisations, such as the Salvation Army, set up soup kitchens to feed the starving poor.

Families without homes were sent to the local parish workhouses. These were grim places which provided basic food and shelter for the poor in return for work. The food was very meagre and consisted mainly of bread and gruel, which contained little nourishment.

▲ White bread became very popular but it lacked the vitamins of brown bread. Many poor people who lived mainly on white bread and margarine suffered from a disease called rickets.

▲ Dinnertime for the women of St Pancras Workhouse, London in 1900.

Gruel

Here is a recipe for gruel, which was often watered down until it had hardly any flavour.

Fry a chopped onion in a tablespoon of suet and season it with cinnamon, salt and pepper. Stir in a dessertspoon of fine oatmeal and mix well. Gradually add milk and/or water until you have a thin sauce. Boil well and serve hot.

Wealthy people, on the other hand, lived very well. They had large houses and lots of servants to cook and clean. Their meals consisted of many courses, eaten at grand dining tables, which were laid out with elegant china, cutlery and glass, and decorated with magnificient table displays. The upper classes 'dressed' for dinner – the gentlemen in suits and black tie, and the ladies in elaborate gowns.

The middle classes also ate well, and would expect at least six different dishes to be served at dinner. Most families had a cook and servants who worked 'below stairs' in the kitchen.

Dinner was the main meal of the day for the rich, and was usually eaten around six o'clock in the evening, though by the end of the century, it became fashionable to eat later.

By the mid-nineteenth century the organisation of the courses at a fashionable meal were finally as we know them today: soup, followed by fish, meat and dessert. Although there was a choice within the courses, there was not a mixture of foods as in earlier times.

People became much more particular about table manners. After dinner, ladies left the gentlemen alone to drink port so that they could have a more 'masculine' conversation. Also, young ladies were advised not to take cheese at the end of the meal because it was 'unladylike'.

Sometimes these table manners became rather silly. In a novel called 'Cranford' written at that time, the author, Mrs Gaskell, refers to two sisters at dinner who retire behind a screen to eat oranges, in case they should offend someone!

41

Victorian recipes

Although there were now shops and bakehouses in the industrial towns, many housewives liked to do their own baking. Pies were a particular favourite at this time. Here is a recipe for a savoury pie made at harvest time.

Fidget pie

Ingredients:
200 gms of shortcrust pastry
3 large onions
5 large potatoes
3 large baking apples
250 gms of bacon
 or 250 gms of ham
salt and pepper
stock (for details of how
 to make stock see the
 recipe for Nettle soup
 on page 7 or, use a
 stock cube to save
 time)

What to do:

1 Grease a pie dish.

2 Fill the dish with thin layers of sliced onions, potato and apple, and strips of bacon or ham.

3 Season the pie filling with salt and pepper and pour stock over it.

4 Cover with pastry, decorate the top with pastry leaves and brush with beaten egg and milk to glaze it.

5 Bake at 400°F, 204°C or Gas Mark 6 for 30 minutes until golden, then cover the top with a double sheet of wet, greaseproof paper, so that the filling continues to cook but so that the pastry does not burn. Bake for a further 30 minutes.

▼ There were many traditional and regional shapes for pies, such as the Cornish pasty. The 'checky pig' from Leicestershire is great fun. Try making a few, filling them with the same ingredients as the Fidget pie, chopped up small to cook more quickly.

Cornish pasty

Checky pig

▲ 'Stargazey' pies were often made using fish such as sardines or pilchards. Here are some of the different ways of making them.

Puddings were very popular in Victorian times. Here is a recipe you might like to try.

Summer pudding

Ingredients:
thin slices of crustless bread
1 kg of soft, red fruits
  (such as raspberries, strawberries, cherries and red or blackcurrants)
2–3 tablespoons of sugar according to taste

What to do:

1 Line a pudding basin with the slices of bread, cut to fit.

2 Put the fruit and sugar in a saucepan and heat until the juice runs.

3 Fill the bread mould with the fruit and cover the top with more slices of bread.

4 Find a plate that just fits over the top of the basin and weight it down. Leave overnight in a refrigerator.

5 Turn out carefully on to a dish and serve with cream.

Several recipe books were written especially for invalids and included foods that were easy to digest, but nutritious. One of these was:

Lemon barley water

Ingredients:
2 tablespoons of pearl barley
2 litres of water
2 lemons

What to do:

1 Wash the pearl barley.

2 Put it in a large pan with the water and bring to the boil.

3 Grate the rind of two lemons and add to the water. Then cover and leave to cool.

4 Squeeze the lemons and add the juice to the pan.

5 Strain the mixture through a sieve and sweeten it to taste.

Real lemonade

If you pour plain, boiled water on to the lemon rind and do not use any barley in the recipe, you will be left with a cheap, refreshing lemonade drink.

Food from India

During Victoria's reign, India became part of the British Empire and many British people lived in India as soldiers, businessmen or administrators. When they returned, they brought Indian recipes home with them. One of these was kedgeree, which was eaten at breakfast time.

Kedgeree

Ingredients:
large knob of butter
a shallot
2 cupfuls long grain rice
  (already cooked)
2 cupfuls smoked haddock
2 eggs (hardboiled)
pinch turmeric
salt and pepper

What to do:

1 Melt a large knob of butter in a frying pan and gently fry the chopped shallot.

2 Stir in 2 cupfuls of cooked, rice, 2 cupfuls of cooked, smoked haddock (flaked into pieces), and season to taste.

3 Sprinkle with turmeric and stir in 2 chopped, hardboiled eggs.

4 Pile the mixture on to a hot dish and serve it decorated with parsley.

The English who returned from India also liked the hot, spicy foods to which they had become accustomed. Chutney was a favourite, and was often used to liven up the leftover Sunday joint, which was served up in different ways throughout the following week.

Apricot and apple chutney
(Get an adult to help you with this.)

Ingredients:
680 gms cooking apples
230 gms dried apricots
2 handfuls of sultanas
6 cloves of garlic (crushed in a garlic crusher)
400 mls of wine vinegar
8 tablespoons of brown sugar
2 teaspoons of salt
$\frac{1}{2}$ teaspoon of cayenne pepper

What to do:

1 Put the cooking apples and the apricots on a wooden board and chop with a sharp knife.

2 Put the apple and apricots into a pan with all the other ingredients.

3 Bring the contents of the pan to the boil, then turn down to medium heat so that they simmer well for about 30 minutes. Stir regularly and turn the heat down to low as the liquid evaporates. The chutney will become quite thick, so make sure it does not stick to the bottom of the pan.

4 Leave to cool, spoon the chutney into a well-cleaned jar and seal with a lid. Make a pretty label for your jar.

Seasonal recipes

There are some entertaining recipes which are linked with seasonal folk customs, many of which were revived by the Victorians.

Gingerbread men were made to decorate the Christmas tree, but they could also be turned into 'Jack-in-the-Green' on Mayday, by decorating the head with a wreath of bright green icing.

Gingerbread men

Ingredients:
250 gms of self-raising flour
a lump of butter
a tablespoon of sugar
2 egg yolks
1 egg white
1 teaspoon of ground ginger
raisins   } for decoration
candied peel }

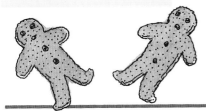

What to do:

1 Put all the ingredients (except the raisins and candied peel) into a bowl, and mix together.

2 When the mixture is fairly solid, use a rolling pin to roll out thinly on a floured board.

3 Cut into gingerbread men shapes (you can buy a special cutter for this).

4 Decorate the gingerbread men with raisins for eyes and candied peel for mouths.

5 Put on a greased baking tray, and bake in a moderate oven (350°F, 180°C, Gas Mark 4) for 10–15 minutes.

After the farm workers had gathered the harvest in safely, the farmer or squire would hold a large harvest supper in his barn to thank everyone. The feast would often include roast pork, rabbit pies, harvest loaves, punch and lemonade.

◀ A traditional Victorian 'Harvest Home'.

Harvest loaf

This is made from bread dough to look like a sheaf of corn. Cut your bread dough into strands and use scissors to snip the dough into ears of corn. Before putting it in the oven, brush the dough with egg yolk beaten with a little milk, so that it will be golden and shiny when baked.

45

Sugar mice

These were often put in the children's Christmas stockings.

Ingredients:
$\frac{1}{4}$ lb of icing sugar
the white of an egg
a few drops of cochineal (if you want a pink mouse)

To decorate:
silver balls
a few sliced almonds
string

What to do:

1 Mix the ingredients so they bind together. (If it seems a bit moist, add a little more icing sugar)

2 Sprinkle some icing sugar on a board and knead the mixture.

3 Break the mixture into several pieces and shape each one into a mouse.

4 Add a piece of string for the tail, silver balls for the eyes and pieces of sliced almond for the ears.

Stained glass windows

Victorian children used to love making these out of bits of pastry and broken boiled sweets.

Ingredients:
leftover pastry
a few boiled sweets

What to do:

1 Line a baking tray with tin foil or baking paper.

2 Use strips of pastry to make the outline of a stained glass window. Seal the joins by brushing with water.

3 Put broken pieces of boiled sweets into the spaces, using a separate colour for each. (Do not mix the colours as they will look muddy.)

4 Bake lightly in a moderate oven (350°F, 180°C, Gas Mark 4). Do not overcook or the colours will all turn brown.

5 Allow to cool and remove very carefully, as they are fragile.

6 Hold your stained glass window up to the light to see all the different colours!

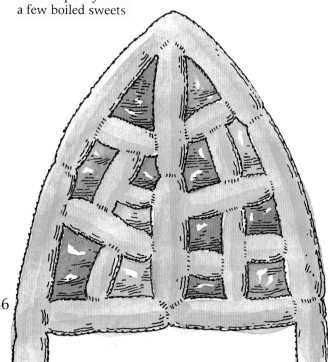

Christmas Eve wigs

On Christmas Eve there was a custom of 'wassailing' the apple trees. This was drinking the health of the trees with cider, so that they would bear good fruit. The hot cider was carried out in a wassail bowl and some of it was sprinkled on the trees. This ritual was supposed to scare away the evil spirits and make the tree bear good fruit the following year.

Christmas Eve 'wigs' were eaten when the apple trees had been wassailed. They were also placed in the branches of the trees to feed the birds, so that they would guard the tree well.

▲ A cartoon taken from the magazine 'Punch', showing the seasonal Wassail Bowl.

Ingredients:

butter or margarine	milk
8 tablespoons of self-raising flour	1 egg
1 dessertspoon of caster sugar	
2 dessertspoons of chopped candied peel	
2 tsps of caraway seeds	

What to do:

1 Put the flour into a bowl. Rub a large knob of butter or margarine into the flour.

2 Mix in the sugar, candied peel and caraway seeds.

3 Beat the egg with a little milk and add to the mixture.

4 Mix to a soft dough.

5 Divide into small lumps and put into the tins.

6 Bake for about 20 minutes in a fairly hot oven (400°F, 204°C, Gas Mark 6), until they are nicely browned.

7 Stand on a wire baking tray, to cool.

Things to do

1 Hold a Victorian harvest supper for your friends. Dress up in a pinafore and bonnet, or cap and waistcoat so as to look the part.

You could serve hot soup with harvest loaf to start, followed by fidget pie and salad. Finish off with apples and cheese and real lemonade.

Try some country dancing or songs.

2 Next Christmas try out some of the recipes in this book and celebrate some of the customs, such as wassailing the apple tree.

An interesting book which tells you all about them is:
Discovering Christmas Customs and Folklore by Margaret Baker (Shire)

47

Index

Bibliography

Here are some other books you may find interesting or
helpful:
  1 *Food and Cooking in Britain* (English Heritage)
(This is a series of seven booklets covering Prehistoric times
and other periods up to the 19th century. They can be bought
as a pack or separately.)
  2 *Food and Cooking* by M Baker (A & C Black)*
  3 *The Story of the Kitchen* by S E Ellacott (Methuen)*
  4 *Food* by S Ferguson (Batsford)*
  5 *Food* by M M Harrison (Ward Lock)*
  6 *Meals through the Ages* by P Moss (Harrap)*
  7 *Christmas and Festive Day Recipes* by S Paston-
      Williams (The National Trust)
  8 *Britain's Food* by P Redmayne (Murray)*

*Children's books

A CIP catalogue record for this book is available from the
British Library.

ISBN 0–7136–3321–2

First published 1991 by A & C Black (Publishers) Limited
35 Bedford Row, London, WC1R 4JH

Text copyright © 1991 Jo Lawrie
Illustrations copyright © 1991 Peter Bailey (Linda Rodgers Associates)
Edited by Carol Watson

Reprinted 1992

Acknowledgements
The publishers would like to thank Lisa Chaney for her
help and advice. Pictures by Bodleian Library pages 15
(both), 19; the Board of Trustees of the V & A, The
Bridgeman Art Library, London page 35; Butser Ancient
Farm page 8; Corpus Christi College, Oxford page 20; The
Hulton Picture Library page 40 (bottom); Mary Evans
Picture Library pages 34, 37 (top and bottom), 38 (bottom),
45; University of Reading, Institute of Agricultural History
and Museum of English Rural Life page 31; Mansell
Collection page 26 (bottom); Museum of London page 30;
Allan Forbes/National Trust for Scotland page 38 (centre);
Natural History Museum, London page 5; Robert Opie
pages 37 (centre), 40 (top); Punch page 47; Sainsbury's
page 38 (top); York Castle Museum page 26 (top).

Filmset by August Filmsetting, Haydock, St Helens
Printed in Hong Kong by Tien Wah Press (Pte.) Ltd